*This Friendship Journal
belongs to*

_____

_____

Date started

_____

Date completed

_____

This *Friendship Journal* is dedicated to my wonderful friends—and I hope I celebrate you and our friendship often enough that you know who you are— as well as my husband Fred, our sons Jeffrey and Scott, and my family members whom I dearly love. This journal is also dedicated to the memory of my father, who kept a journal during his 64th year, a treasure that he left for me to read and share, and to my late brother, whose poetry and plays that he left behind are like his literary journals.

Other Journals by Jan Yager, Ph.D.
Birthday Book: A Journal
Personal Journal: Blank Book With Ruled Pages
Everything Notebook: Business Journal/Blank Book With Ruled Pages
The Time to Lose Journal

Selected Other Books by Jan Yager, Ph.D. (a/k/a J.L. Barkas)
Friendshifts®: The Power of Friendship and How It Shapes Our Lives
Friendship: A Selected, Annotated Bibliography
Creative Time Management for the New Millennium
Creative Time Management
Making Your Office Work for You
Business Protocol: How to Survive & Succeed in Business
Effective Business & Nonfiction Writing
Victims
The Cantaloupe Cat: A Picture Book (illustrated by Mitzi Lyman)
Untimely Death: A Novel (co-authored with Fred Yager)

Friendship Journal

Selected Quotes About Friendship From *Friendshifts*®
and a Journal

Cover art, interior design, introduction,
self-quizzes, directories, and quotations
by

Jan Yager, Ph.D.

(Author of *Friendshifts:*®
The Power of Friendship and How It Shapes Our Lives)

Hannacroix Creek Books, Inc.   **Stamford, CT**

Published by: Hannacroix Creek Books, Inc.
               1127 High Ridge Road
               PMB #110
               Stamford, Connecticut 06905-1203 U.S.A.
               (203) 321-8674   Fax (203) 968-0193

Visit us on the web: http://www.Hannacroix.com
               E-mail: Hannacroix@aol.com

Printed in the United States

Introduction by Dr. Jan Yager

Journals are a gift you give to yourself or someone else--the gift of recording, remembering, and sharing. I still have the first journal I began when I was ten years old. Whether this is your first journal, or your 50th, keeping a journal is a wonderful tool for self-discovery. This friendship journal could provide you with the place to share your thoughts and feelings about your friendships. You could use this friendship journal as a daily diary or you could only write in it when the spirit moves you.

This could be a general journal for you in which you record or work through everyone and anything in your life and work. Or you might want to focus on friendship and your friends, the theme that is addressed in the quotes excerpted from my book *Friendshifts®: The Power of Friendship and How It Shapes Our Lives* (Stamford, CT: Hannacroix Creek Books, 2nd edition, 1999; originally published, 1997. That book is based on the two decades of original research I have been doing on friendship, dating back to my sociology dissertation on friendship patterns (City University of New York, 1983).

It was quite a challenging task to distill almost 300 pages of research, examples, and anecdotes into just 100 or so quotes! Of course I hope you will add your own friendship thoughts , quotes, comments, or observations to the ones included on these pages.

The selected quotes from *Friendshifts®* are reprinted at the top of each page so you have lots of space available for your own thoughts, writing, or notetaking. I also have included in the back of this friendship journal 7 ways to make time for your friends as well as a self-quiz about current friendships., reprinted from *Friendshifts®.* Completely new for this journal, however, I created a "Friendship Self-evaluation" that could help you zone in on who your current friends are and whether or not you are communicating with them as often as you would like as well as how you celebrate each other's birthdays or any other traditions you are developing as friends.

Also at the back of this *Friendship Journal* is a telephone directory where you could put key contact information to facilitate staying in communication with your friends as well as a gift or card list for recording what you send to, or receive from, your friends.

Perhaps you plan to give a blank, new version of this journal to a friend, parent, sibling, child, spouse, or romantic partner for a birthday or holiday gift. Perhaps you plan to fill in the journal and give a completed one to a treasured friend as a legacy of your friendship.

Or perhaps you plan to keep this journal for yourself as part of your personal legacy. Whatever you plan to do with this journal, enjoy the glorious road of self-awareness and self-discovery that it will inspire in its author.

To further highlight the importance of friendship, and provide a one week long celebration of this unique, often misunderstood crucial personal relationship, I founded National New Friends, Old Friends Week. It occurs the Sunday after Mother's Day, each May, and lasts till the following Saturday. You will find out more information about National New Friends, Old Friends Week at my web sites:

http://www.JanYager.com
http://www.JanYager.com/friendship.

Here are two other web sites that deal with keeping a journal:

www.whole-heart.com
Whole Heart publications

www.journaltherapy.com
The Center for Journal Therapy

Jan Yager, Ph.D.
P.O. Box 8038
Stamford, CT 06905-8038
http://www.JanYager.com

> *Genuine friends are willing to be there for you; they do not just make hollow offers. ***

*All the printed quotes in this *Friendship Journal* are by Dr. Jan Yager. These quotes are excerpted, with permission, from Dr. Yager's book, *Friendshifts®: The Power of Friendship and How It Shapes Our Lives* (Hannacroix Creek Books, 2nd edition, 1999, 287 pages), available in trade paperback or hardcover at your local library, or for sale through your local or on-line bookstores, through the web site http://www. Hannacroix.com, or , prepaid, by calling 1-800-431-1579.

You have to be careful to avoid assuming your friends are "mind readers" about what your emotional needs are at any given time, or that they are even aware of what you might be going through. Sometimes they may be unaware of what you are going through or that it has such an effect on you. If they did, they might reach out.

_____

_____

_____

_____

_____

_____

_____

_____

_____

_____

_____

_____

_____

_____

_____

_____

_____

_____

_____

_____

_____

_____

One way to define friend *is by the level of intimacy in the relationship. The three categories of friends are best, close, or casual friends.*

Even if you are lucky enough to be raised in a very responsive and loving family, it is inevitable that you will someday leave home. But friends--old friends whom you have cultivated over the years, or newer ones whom you develop in your new communities--will always be available to you for affirmation and companionship.

If you do have a mate or romantic partner, it is ideal to be best friends with your mate as well as lovers. However, even when you attain that ideal, you need platonic friends where shared income, living arrangements, or the roles of spouse or parent are less likely to complicate the relationship.

The wish to become friends needs to be shared or the relationship will stop in its tracks.

Even children need guidance in how to develop and maintain friends.

Friendshifts® are inevitable; as our lives change, so do our friendships. Moving a friendship to a different level of intensity or frequency, or even letting it fade away, does not diminish what that relationship once gave you.

As your life gets busier or more compartmentalized, it is too easy to discount how essential friendship is for you, whatever your age or marital status.

Some are afraid to admit that friends play a factor in their professional success; they fear people will think they got where they are just because of their friends, not their talents. Yet in reality, both talent and friends are usually needed.

The right friends can help you feel worthwhile. The right friends can even help get you elected president. School, work, parenting, and even old age are better and more fun when shared with friends.

> I'm made up of the people I know and the friends I keep. I'd be nothing without them.
> --*20-year-old Penn State male freshman*

A truism about friendship is that it is an optional role. The other necessary roles--of worker, of spouse, or of parent-- have to be satisfied first. If friendship interferes with performing those roles, it just might have to be put on hold or eliminated.

Whether the need to form new friends is caused by a change in interests, a move to another city, a promotion to another level or into another profession, or the death of old friends or even of a spouse, shifting to new friendships that serve current needs makes it possible to feel connected even if old friends are seen less frequently, if at all.

Friendshifts® *is a word coined for the way our friendships change as we go from one stage in our life to another, or even relocate from one school, job, neighborhood, or community to another. It is a variation on the old adage "Make new friends but keep the old; one is silver, but the other's gold."*

Behind friendship is the nice or likability factor. A key way to have friends is to be likable and interested in others.

Friends can be a source of self-esteem, affection, and good times.

Friends can offset the low self-esteem and loneliness caused by abusive or dysfunctional families before, or in addition to, intervention by therapists or family services.

> **Friendship.** *It's something many people take for granted. They are unaware how powerful and positive friendship can be, or they would take it more seriously.*

_____

_____

_____

_____

_____

_____

_____

_____

_____

_____

_____

_____

_____

_____

_____

_____

_____

_____

_____

_____

_____

_____

_____

Celebrate *your friend's triumphs. Though competitive feelings are normal, deal with yours so it does not sabotage your friendship.*

_____

_____

_____

_____

_____

_____

_____

_____

_____

_____

_____

_____

_____

_____

_____

_____

_____

_____

_____

_____

_____

_____

_____

_____

What all these friendships have in common, however, whether you are talking about a best, close, or casual friend, is that the friendship would exist even if the circumstances under which the relationship was formed ended. For example, you leave your job or move, but your co-worker or neighbor is still your friend. Unlike the acquaintances that languish, best, close, or casual friendships are maintained, even if the relationship becomes less convenient.

No matter what your house looks like, you let friends in.
--*Mary Kent, photographer*

Although writing is a one-sided communication, and it is time consuming, it offers a chance for sharing, connecting, closeness, and communication that friendships, even face-to-face or phone friendships, sometimes lack.

By and large, however, best, close, and casual friends are somewhat like the differences among dating, engagement, and marriage, with casual friend at the bottom of the scale, in terms of intimacy, and best friend at the top.

Another way to define friend *is to say it is someone who is there if you are in need. But today, everyone seems to be more concerned with either job, spouse, or children.... Besides, the notion of a friend in need is somewhat*

Best friendship is the kind of friendship that conjures up the strongest fantasies about friendship--someone who is there for you, no matter what, someone who puts you first in his or her life. This person is the friend, before all others; it is a relationship that has withstood the tests of time and conflict, major changes such as moving, or status changes, such as marrying or having a child.

Friendship, like love, requires an investment of time and effort.

> Friendship is a virtue.
> --Aristotle, *The Nicomachean Ethics*

Keep your view of your friends up-to-date; avoid outdated and unrealistic perceptions based on outdated information.

> *As the number of friendships in each category—best, close, or casual—increases, the value of each relationship may decrease, as well as its members' dependence on it.*

_____
_____
_____
_____
_____
_____
_____
_____
_____
_____
_____
_____
_____
_____
_____
_____
_____
_____
_____
_____
_____
_____
_____

There is usually a "chemical" reaction--a connection--to each other that makes you feel you want to get to know that person better and to perhaps become his or her friend.

Close friends are faithful, dear, tender, reliable, and intimate. It is close friends, especially outside the workplace--not best or casual--who offer you the choice relationship outside of romance or family ties to fulfill your emotional or intellectual needs.

Respect your friends' boundaries.

A casual friend is the kind of friendship that is becoming synonymous with friend *for today's busy women or men and for those who feel they have too much to lose by "telling all" in a best or close friendship.*

> *One way that you might define a* friend *is by those qualities that are sought in a friend, such as commitment, self-disclosure, trust, honesty, and commonality.*

As relationships become more intimate, the information shared becomes more personal. That is why, even in the best romantic relationships, interacting with friends, including casual ones, may benefit a couple.

Shared values are more important in predicting the longevity of a friendship than shared interests.

Friendships are the crown jewels that one owns. The stock market might go up and down, but friendships only grow in their value. —*78-year-old Gladys Barkas*

Although the wish to become friends must be shared by both acquaintances, what you share need not be equal. "All my friends leave it up to me to be the one to pick up the phone," says Debbie.

The change in reasons—from a generalized wish to have a friend, to that friend's specific attributes—is notable because unless that shift occurs, the friendship will end when there are conflicts, or a loss of physical proximity.

A best or close friendship that becomes less intimate may be more difficult to maintain than a casual one that remains for decades at a more superficial level.

There are two elements that go to the composition of
friendship...One is Truth...The other element of
friendship is tenderness. -- Ralph Waldo Emerson,
"Friendship," *Essays* (1841)

The notion in friendship that like attracts like is ancient; now, social scientists are supporting that axiom with experiments, observations, survey research, and data analysis.

Changes, such as moving up or down the corporate ladder, should not impact old friendships, since friends connect on a deeper basis.

Avoid misusing friends as therapists or banks.

> *The ingredients for an acquaintance to become a friend
> include: visibility; access; expanding your interaction
> beyond the original basis on which you and your
> acquaintance first met and interacted; and fourth, is time.*

It takes, on average, three years from the time two people meet and became acquaintances until a genuine tried-and-true friendship develops. The time frame of three years from meeting a new person to becoming tried-and-true friends makes sense; by that time, most acquaintances are no longer convenient. Someone may have graduated, switched schools, gotten a promotion, changed jobs, moved away, gotten married or divorced, or had a child. All those changes are "tests" of your relationship.

Here are ways to help an acquaintanceship to become a friendship:

- *Show an interest in your acquaintance's life—family, work, hobbies, and personal concerns.*
- *Avoid gossiping about your acquaintance.*
- *Remember your acquaintance's birthday or any other key upcoming anniversaries or special occasions.*
- *Return phone calls promptly.*
- *Communicate with each other, and see each other, on a regular basis.*
- *Emphasize shared values and interests.*

> *Too often friendships, especially long-standing ones, are taken for granted until it is too late.*

What are the most frequent reasons an acquaintance becomes a friend? Besides having a shared desire to become friends, the most frequent reason is if you think your future friend will offer companionship—someone to do things with *or* talk to. *The next most common reason is* shared interests, *followed by the belief that your friend will offer you* emotional support.

> *The good news is that while friendship may be a repetition of past familial relationships, it may also be an opportunity to work on, and even improve, those early interactions.*

Friendships primarily based on **emotional support** *are, predictably, more intense and uneven than those based on doing things together, talking, or shared interests.*

There is also a very important factor to consider in why an acquaintance may become a friend, namely **the fun factor.** *Since there are usually other relationships in your acquaintance's life to turn to for emotional support, information, advice, or help, one of the most sought-after qualities in a friend is the ability to "have fun together."*

> *"I cannot have a friendship without having honesty and loyalty."* --21-year-old female college senior

_____

_____
_____
_____
_____
_____
_____
_____
_____
_____
_____
_____
_____
_____
_____
_____
_____
_____
_____
_____
_____
_____
_____
_____
_____
_____
_____
_____
_____

Whether or not you do lean on your friends during a crisis, you should feel that, if you wanted to, you could.

_____

_____

_____

_____

_____

_____

_____

_____

_____

_____

_____

_____

_____

_____

_____

_____

_____

_____

_____

_____

_____

_____

_____

_____

_____

_____

_____

_____

> "It used to be that I had five days that I could fill up with seeing friends, and now [since I'm married] maybe I have one. So I concentrate very carefully."
> --31-year-old publicist married for one year

Couples need to make finding time for friends a key concern in their lives, including new friends they meet together, whose friendships they share.

_____
_____
_____
_____
_____
_____
_____
_____
_____
_____
_____
_____
_____
_____
_____
_____
_____
_____
_____
_____
_____
_____
_____
_____
_____

Friends are vital for new mothers; they may help prevent you from making excessive emotional demands on your spouse. This is especially true if you are suddenly removed from the work environment that used to nurture and support you, and you have not yet created an alternative satisfying "at-home mother" lifestyle.

There is an adage that to have a friend, be a friend, but what kind of friend should you be?

> *Coming through for others when they are going through the terminal illness or death of a loved one may not guarantee you are, or will become, better friends, but failing to come through may stop that relationship in its tracks.*

_____

_____

_____

_____

_____

_____

_____

_____

_____

_____

_____

_____

_____

_____

_____

_____

_____

_____

_____

_____

_____

_____

_____

_____

_____

_____

_____

The more you sincerely listen to your friends, the more your friends are pulled toward you.

_____
_____
_____
_____
_____
_____
_____
_____
_____
_____
_____
_____
_____
_____
_____
_____
_____
_____
_____
_____
_____
_____
_____
_____
_____

Being sympathetic toward your friend's point of view or situation, and showing empathy, is one way to achieve better listening skills. It is too easy to impose your viewpoint—your experiences—rather than to understand where your friend is coming from.

> *Trust means your friend is there for you. It also means if you reveal private thoughts or information or share something confidential, it is not revealed.*

The way self-disclosures, or confessions, are handled in a friendship will certainly affect the trust friends feel about each other. Although self-disclosures may occur early in a friendship, they usually emerge as friends develop a shared history, and the friendship is moved along from casual to close or best.

Alternatives to self-disclosure to a friend are writing in a journal or diary, introspection, therapy, confessing to a member of the clergy, or attending self-help support groups where you disclose to strangers with anonymity, the cornerstone of most groups' foundation.

> *Ideally, a friendship is maintained because your needs are being met by the relationship, and there is a shared desire to perpetuate, or even deepen, it.*

So if envy or even jealousy are "normal," just because a friend is envious or jealous of you, or vice versa, should not automatically rule out that friendship. Even very close friends may be jealous at times. The fact that jealousy rarely occurs, or that you or your friend acknowledge and deal with those feelings, helps define them as friends rather than "everyone else."

Closeness also makes you vulnerable. Being close opens you up to the potential for loss and pain.

> *Trust is one of the most meaningful traits you can find in a best or close, and even a casual, friend.*

My mother used to have a wonderful saying that I've adopted, which she would sometimes pull out on holidays. She would drink a toast to us and say, "It's so nice to like the ones you love." *--Nella Barkley, president, Crystal/Barkley*

> What could be finer than to have someone to whom you
> may speak as freely as to yourself?
> --*Cicero, "On Friendship"*

> In my happiest days, my wife is my best friend. In my saddest days, my wife is my best friend. She's the one I can share all my thoughts with.
> --*William Barkas, D.D.S., married 54 years*

> I consider my brothers and sister friends I take for granted. —*45-year-old married New Jersey man*

I consider my children my friends. We feel very close to each other. —*72-year-old Westchester married woman*

When siblings get along like the best of friends, they offer each other the potential for a textured and powerful friendship; they share one of the most exalted aspects of long-standing friendships, namely a shared history.

> *Becoming closer with your mother or father may help you become more comfortable with intimacy in all the other key relationships in your life.*

Pets offer friendship in place of, or in addition to, peers. Indeed, the care that pets require may just be what is necessary for a child to learn the give and take that most friendships entail. Becoming sensitive to the nonverbal and verbal cues of a pet may enable a child or adult to become a more aware and giving friend.

One of the reasons friendship is so magical and so potentially rewarding: it allows connections that permit a window into the deepest core and essence of another.

> *Of course you are allowed to be busy, but if your friends want to get together, being busy too often and for too extended a period may result in fading or ending those friendships.*

_____
_____
_____
_____
_____
_____
_____
_____
_____
_____
_____
_____
_____
_____
_____
_____
_____
_____
_____
_____
_____
_____
_____
_____
_____
_____

> *Recognizing the limitations of friendship may help you make fewer unrealistic demands on your friends and, hence, salvage friendships that might have ended.*

One of the many ways to feel significant within yourself is to go the distance for others; to come through even when it puts you out; to help your friend, or your mother, spouse, or sibling, when it is tough for you, when it involves a sacrifice of your time, energy, and personal needs and goals, when it is downright inconvenient, difficult, time-consuming, or even expensive to do so.

Since the only person you can be assured of changing is yourself, start there.

One way that you might define a friend is by those qualities
that are sought in a friend, such as commitment, self-
disclosure, trust, honesty, and commonality.

Regular get-togethers are the best way for a friend to stay current and not stuck in the past.

_____

_____

_____

_____

_____

_____

_____

_____

_____

_____

_____

_____

_____

_____

_____

_____

_____

_____

_____

_____

_____

_____

_____

_____

_____

_____

_____

_____

_____

Friendships that last either have less conflict than those that end or involve friends who know, or have learned, how to effectively handle conflict.

Being discreet is essential with all types of work friendships.

> *The friendship factor in marriage (or any intimate romantic relationship) depends on trusting each other, committing to each other and to the marriage (romantic relationship), and spending time together.*

The best way to facilitate becoming a friend with your children when they become adults is to spend time with them when they are young, getting to know each other, building a shared history and pleasant memories to be called up for review and reminiscing throughout your lives.

Friendship is an untapped source of help for dysfunctional families—in childhood and adult years—and in that way, friendship might compensate for what was (or is) missing at home.

_____
_____
_____
_____
_____
_____
_____
_____
_____
_____
_____
_____
_____
_____
_____
_____
_____
_____
_____
_____
_____
_____
_____
_____
_____
_____
_____
_____
_____
_____

> *Success in many careers is based on relationship building, and nothing builds a trusting relationship faster than the elusive and magical relationship known as friendship.*

Additional tips for maintaining and improving friendships:
- *Make getting together with friends, especially best or close ones, a key concern, up there along with work, family, other relatives, hobby, or sports interests.*
- *Use the holidays to catch up with friends and to show them they matter, whether that means a phone call, a personalized card or letter, an appropriate gift, or a visit.*

If you like yourself, you will more easily find others who want to be with you as well.

> *We have more relationship choices than any other generation has ever had; our best, close, or casual friendships potentially could benefit from those shifts.*

FRIENDSHIP SELF-QUIZ*

Consider asking yourself these eight questions about your close or best friendships to assess the current quality of the friendship:

1. Do you and your friend communicate -- by phone, fax, letters, or e-mail -- or get together as often as you and your friend want to?
2. Do you and your friend have fun together?
3. When you and your friend speak on the phone, or get together, do you feel connected and appreciated by your friend?
4. Is this friendship basically reciprocal (rather than one way)?
5. Do you and your friend share the same values on issues that matter to you both or, if you do not, are these value disparities easily overlooked?
6. Do you like this friend?
7. Has this friendship stood the test of time and structural changes such as graduating, moving, getting married, switching jobs, or having children?
8. Is conflict with this friend minimal or, if it does occur, are you able to resolve it without long-term resentment?

*

If you answered "no" to one or more of the above questions about a particular friendship, it may indicate that you or your friend need to do some work on your relationship.

*Excerpted, with permission, from page 126 of *Friendshifts®: The Power of Friendship and How It Shapes Our Lives* by Dr. Jan Yager (Hannacroix Creek Books, www.Hannacroix.com, 2nd edition, 1999).

Here are some ways to keep up with your friends, no matter how busy you are*:

1. Keep postcards with you so if you have a spare moment while waiting in the doctor's office, sitting around while your child is taking guitar lessons or playing soccer, while commuting, or away on a business trip, so you can use those moments to write to your friends, especially your out-of-town friends, bringing them up to date on your news and keeping in contact.

2. Consider having a holiday celebration for just friends the day after Thanksgiving if you spend Thanksgiving with your relatives. Take turns alternating what friend is responsible for the food or have everyone bring along a dish or beverage. Include the same friends each year or invite different friends from year-to-year.

3. Plan to meet at the neighborhood supermarket or drive together, or meet, and shop together at a local or far away store or mall.

4. Have the phone numbers, addresses, E-mail addresses, and schedules of your friends handy so you can easily call or send a note or E-mail whenever you want to.

5. Make a commitment to get together on a regular basis, depending upon time and distance, on your own or with your spouses or families.

6. Remember your friend's birthday by calling, sending a card, or getting together. Here are a few gift ideas: a picture frame; a book; a journal; or a store or restaurant gift certificate.

7. Volunteer to work in a soup kitchen, tutor children, spend time with the elderly in assisted living communities, read to elementary school children, or tutor together with your friend.

*Excerpted, with permission, from the 31 ways to keep up with your friends suggested on pages 214-218 of *Friendshifts®: The Power of Friendship and How It Shapes Our Lives* by Dr. Jan Yager (Hannacroix Creek Books, 2nd edition, 1999).

Friendship Evaluations

MY CLOSE OR BEST FRIENDS ARE:

1. _____
2. _____
3. _____
4. _____
5. _____
6. _____
7. _____
8. _____
9. _____
10. _____

THE LAST TIME I SAW _____ (friend #1)
was _____ hours/days/weeks/years ago.

We get together
Often _____   Occasionally _____
Rarely _____   Seldom _____
Never _____

I/we would like to see (speak) to each other
_____ more frequently _____ less often _____ it's fine now.
Action plan for spending more time with_____ (friend #1):

1. _____
2. _____
3. _____
4. _____

Friend #1's birthday is: _____

We celebrate by: _____
_____ calling   _____ sending a card
_____ sending/giving a gift   _____ getting together

_____ other _____

Any other traditions with _____ (friend #1):

_____

NATIONAL NEW FRIENDS, OLD FRIENDS WEEK
BEGINS ON the Sunday after Mother's Day each year till the
following Saturday.
CELEBRATE WITH YOUR FRIENDS!
For more information on friendship and on this friendship
celebration, National New Friends, Old Friends Week, visit
this web site:
http://www.JanYager.com/friendship

THE LAST TIME I SAW #2 _____ was
_____ hours/days/weeks/years ago.

We get together
Often _____   Occasionally _____
Rarely _____   Seldom _____
Never _____

I/we would like to see (speak) to each other
_____ more frequently _____ less often _____ it's fine now.
Action plan for spending more time with_____ (friend #2):

1. _____

2. _____

3. _____
4. _____

Friend #2's birthday is: _____

We celebrate by: _____
_____ calling   _____ sending a card
_____ sending/giving a gift   _____ getting together
_____ other _____

Any other traditions with _____ (friend #2):
_____

THE LAST TIME I SAW _____ (friend #3)
was _____ hours/days/weeks/years ago.

We get together
Often _____   Occasionally _____
Rarely _____   Seldom _____
Never _____

I/we would like to see (speak) to each other
_____ more frequently _____ less often _____ it's fine
now.
Action plan for spending more time with_____ (friend #3):

1. _____
2. _____
3. _____
4. _____

Friend #3's birthday is: _____

We celebrate by: _____
_____ calling   _____ sending a card
_____ sending/giving a gift   _____ getting together

_____ other _____

Any other traditions with _____ (friend #3):

_____

THE LAST TIME I SAW _____ (friend #4)
was _____ hours/days/weeks/years ago.

We get together
Often _____   Occasionally _____
Rarely _____   Seldom _____
Never _____

I/we would like to see (speak) to each other
_____ more frequently _____ less often _____ it's fine
now.
Action plan for spending more time with_____ (friend #4):

1. _____
2. _____
3. _____
4. _____

Friend #4's birthday is: _____

We celebrate by: _____
_____ calling   _____ sending a card
_____ sending/giving a gift   _____ getting together
_____ other _____

Any other traditions with _____ (friend #4):

Contact/Telephone Directory

Name
Address
Phone
E-mail

Name
Address
Phone
E-mail

Name
Address
Phone
E-mail

Name
Address
Phone
E-mail

Name
Address
Phone
E-mail

Name
Address
Phone
E-mail

Name
Address
Phone
E-mail

Contact/Telephone Directory

Name
Address
Phone
E-mail

Name
Address
Phone
E-mail

Name
Address
Phone
E-mail

Name
Address
Phone
E-mail

Name
Address
Phone
E-mail

Name
Address
Phone
E-mail

Name
Address
Phone
E-mail

Contact/Telephone Directory

Name
Address
Phone
E-mail

Name
Address
Phone
E-mail

Name
Address
Phone
E-mail

Name
Address
Phone
E-mail

Name
Address
Phone
E-mail

Name
Address
Phone
E-mail

Name
Address
Phone
E-mail

Contact/Telephone Directory

Name
Address
Phone
E-mail

Name
Address
Phone
E-mail

Name
Address
Phone
E-mail

Name
Address
Phone
E-mail

Name
Address
Phone
E-mail

Name
Address
Phone
E-mail

Name
Address
Phone
E-mail

SENDING RECORD

Cards/Gifts
(Birthday/Holiday/Anniversary)

NAME	DATE/YEAR SENT	ITEM (PRESENT/CARD)	OCCASION

SENDING RECORD

Cards/Gifts
(Birthday/Holiday/Anniversary)

NAME	DATE/YEAR SENT	ITEM (PRESENT/CARD)	OCCASION

RECEIVING RECORD

Cards/Gifts
(Birthday/Holiday/Anniversary)

NAME	DATE/YEAR RECEIVED	ITEM (PRESENT/CARD)	OCCASION

RECEIVING RECORD

Cards/Gifts
(Birthday/Holiday/Anniversary)

NAME	DATE/YEAR RECEIVED	ITEM (PRESENT/CARD)	OCCASION

www.ingramcontent.com/pod-product-compliance
Lightning Source LLC
Chambersburg PA
CBHW031220290326
41931CB00035B/562